1999

Little Lord Shiva

The Berkeley Poems, 1968

Little Lord Shiva

The Berkeley Poems, 1968

Charles Potts

with an introduction by

Hugh Fox

Glass Eye Books　　　Northampton, Massachusetts

ISBN: 0-9673832-0-X

Glass Eye Books
PO Box 627
Northampton, MA 01061

Acknowledgments:

Some of the poems in the first section, published as *Little Lord Shiva* by John Oliver Simon and Richard Krech at Noh Directions Press in Berkeley, California, 1969, were first published in *Aldebaran Review*, *The Anthology* (Of Poems Read at COSMEP Berkeley, 1968), *Avalanche*, *Grass Prophet Review*, and *Litmus*. Words are inadequate to express my gratitude and thanks to John Oliver Simon and Richard Krech. These men, they are my brothers. Many of these poems were later collected in *The Golden Calf*, published by Litmus Inc. in Salt Lake City in 1975 and in *Rocky Mountain Man*, published by Harry Smith, to whom great thanks is also due, at The Smith in New York City in 1978, from which several poems in the second section, written in Berkeley but not published in *LLS*, are also taken. "Salvage," "The End," "The Road to Charlie's House," and "The Return of Laffing Water" were first published in *Valga Krusa*, *The Yellow Christ* and *Shit Crackers*, by Litmus Inc. in Salt Lake City in 1977 with great help from its President, Sherm W. Clow, and C.S. Crowther at Wasatch Printing. Thanks to Douglas Blazek and Karl Kempton for help with the tape of "The End." "Aztec Reflector" originally appeared in *Blue up the Nile* from Quixote Press in Madison, Wisconsin, in 1972, published by Morris Edelson and Rich Mangelsdorff. The drawing on page 31 is by Lorelei Bosserman. The drawing on page 51 is by Hanako. "Para Olga" was included in the anthology, *Editor's Choice*, by Morty Sklar from The Spirit That Moves Us Press in Iowa City, Iowa, 1980. *Little Lord Shiva: The Berkeley Poems, 1968*, collects all the extant poetry and songs written by Charles Potts in or near Berkeley at that time except for fragments in disorderly and untyped notebooks and *The Trancemigraçion of Menzu*, published in 1973 by Empty Elevator Shaft in San Francisco, where it was written by the way, at The Tenth Muse Bookstore, and collected in *Rocky Mountain Man*. A half dozen poems written for to and or about the late Patricia Parker are here published for the first time.

books by

Charles Potts

I see the headlights on my aunt's car which means
shortly that I will be going to the movies to see Julie Andrews
in *The Star*. It seems weird them actually going to the moon.
Man is not going to the moon. Three men are going to the moon.
Captain Jim Corbett on cereal packages in my yuth. That's a nice
way to spell yuth. Why can't I go to the moon. I mean right now.
Be there smiling to welcome them. Waving a little green flag and
giving everybody on earth the bird. I'm sure I'm an alien. I wasn't
meant to be here. I'm a spiritual body. Can't keep my feet on the
ground. Want to fly fly away.

Table of Contents

The 1969 edition from **Noh Directions Press**

Introduction

by Hugh Fox
East Lansing, Michigan
March 22, 1999

You walk into *Little Lord Shiva* and you're back in Berkeley in 1968, right in the middle of the psychedelic, visionary, shamanic, flowered/flowering, love-in, be-in world where Charles Potts vanished and then reappeared as Laffing Water:

> Charles Potts is dead...
> My name is Laffing Water
> And whatever form it takes
> I have plenty of...

It was a time filled with an overflowing sense of personal divinity/immortality:

> I'm so motherfucking divine
> I sit on God's right hand
> I am he who am who is.

You were shamanistically transformed by a sacred drug literally into a seer (see-er), filled with a sense of ultimate clarities:

> 4 score and 20 tokes ago
> I entered in
> To the 4th dimension....time

Stopped and everything
Was clear.

Everything is spiritual revolution/revelation, and even a simple thing like taking a piss becomes a mystical experience:

My head stares through my eyes
At my reflection in the toilet
And the piss hit the water
And the image broke
And it began to sing...

Life is a kind of perpetual state of unfolding beatitude. You slide into Laffing Water's and you could just as well be in the mind of Buddha, San Juan de la Cruz or an Aztec initiate who has just taken a dose of Teonanacatl mushrooms, the Flesh of the Gods:

The road to Charlie's house is marked
With only one restriction:
It's rumored Charlie died last night
And the rest is superstition....

He got busted once too hard
Into a million pieces
And ants came dancing 2 by 6
And overran his species.

I'll sing their song with a loud guitar
My voice again tonight.
Charlie's rainbow broke at last
And everything is light.

Noh Directions Press

First Edition Text, 1969

The Nitty Gritty

I'm so motherfucking divine
I sit on God's right hand
I am he who am who is.

I'm the greatest
Mediocre poet
Of my time.

Everything I write is
So so.
I never get high any more.

I've got an answer for everything
Even faintly resembling
Authority and control
Must be destroyed
Immediately.

And one question
For everybody:

Are you with me
Or against me?

You Are My Sunshine

Peepee luck
We used to play.
Our bodies live forever.

I can make you
Savior.

It's hard to be a star
But I just took
My first step
In all directions.

Bring me the middle
Of something nice.

I think
I'd like
Your heart.

Tantrum

The hair is falling out
Of the head I used
To bang on the floor
When nobody listened
To what I had to say.

Poke holes in the wallpaper.
Put on my snow suit.
Go to Grandma Coburn's trailer
For raisins and cheese

Though my mother did buy me
A Zenith record player
In the post war opulence
'Cause I dug the music
And gave me ahead of time
The books she'd bought me
For Christmas
And Years later
Would always fix
My favorite breakfast
Fried pork chops with biscuits and gravy
When I came home from college.

She blew it one day
As I explained to a friend
How I dodged the draft
By saying:
You could still go in
If you wanted to.

Maybe she meant
I was not really crazy
And saw me simply
As a social extension
See the lovely medals and
Where is your boy?

Home is where you go
When there's nothing else happening
We sang as we drank
Our way happily through high school
Where I never was able to
Fuck Mariann,
My virgin of the Main Theatre
Selling popcorn and coke
And holding out
For marriage,
Later made Snow Queen
At Idaho State
Possibly a stewardi
On a 747.

And I never got into
Suzy's pants either,
Little brown migrant
Potato picker
But took her a duck
I didn't want to clean
And watched as she
Plucked off the feathers
And smiled at me

The farmer's son
Who loved anything
Dark and warm.

Watched my friend
Who taught me how to jack off
Put his cock into the milking machine.
Even got my rocks off
Once on the power
Steering
Wheel of a tractor.

Cows
Horses

4-H calves
Colts, lambs and chicken
My hand
Your ass
Her face
Their cunts
Over MYF chili
At the parsonage
Near God's tiny white house
Where I led them in song
And Reverend Fleming complained
When I failed to show up
Being unreasonably detained
For drunk and disorderly
As though I were the
Mistake on
Nature.

Though my friend and I
Accidentally tore the side out
Of his trailer house
With a truckload of fence posts
When he swerved on the hiway
And failed
To as much as slow down
Or recognize
He was the one guilty of
Hit and run,

Later when he came back
To report it
And encourage in fear
The city fathers to cut
Down the gigantic cottonwood trees
That grew in front of
The community Church
Lest they fall on someone
On their way to and from
God's hour a week

Congregation
Who'll never understand

The one song I keep
Singing over and over.
As the star comes together
Near Orion's belt
The waves on the beach
Bring each other in
And I go down
And listen
To the water
Wash the crabs around
To the place it all came from
And let it go again.

Before the beginning
Was nature,
After the end
Will be nature
Never ending.

Now I'm on your side
"Nothing gets closer."
It's like being high
All the time.
As my life approaches
The floating zone
Chaos is verb
And everything moves
To the unchanging standard.

Nature
Keep spinning
Gas into stars
To shine for me
When my light
Is gone.

Para Olga

Ox Carts
Huge wooden wheels
Turn
But not smoothly

Jerking the cart along
The hiway.
Blonde animals pull
With their foreheads
Yoked together,
A team of primary love,
Animals and transportation.
The cart man lumbers
Alongside
The Mercedes-Benz

Busses,
A diesel practical way to jump
Time blocks in El Salvador
Much is moving
To an older beat.
The circle of love closes
A rectangular field of cotton pickers
Hand pulled fibre
A generous ground
And wire retainers
At sundown.

The Negro boy stuffing
A gunny sack
Up the right of way
Stooped
As a gleaner.

The weeds along the road
Bearing as much lost cotton
As the field held naturally
Blown off of trucks
And careless allotments.
He gleans in the evening
A hungry smile and his nimble
Fingers gather the growth
Trans
Planted there
Is no sound but the vibes
From the field hands
Picking their way towards
Night.

*

A ten year old girl tried to sell me
An armadillo
Running alongside
The car in the hills out of Taxco,
The armadillo's feet
Trussed up with string.
She pleads:
Viente viente

Her ragged eyes on the pesos.
The armadillo was not
Struggling
But hung by the string
And swayed back and forth
In the bargain.

*

Candied mangoes
Relleños and black beans
The Pension Gallinda

And the guide who spoke English
Bringing the frumpy tourist ladies
From Guatemala out
To market day at
Chichicastenango

Rapped with me
About the revolution.
Carl, the Latvian old revolutionary
And me neophytic
Listened at the sense he made
Of the fires
On the plain from the hiway.

We thought they were clearing land
By burning.
Montenegro had promised
To burn the country
Running as he was against
Two generals from
Humble Oil.
Got a majority in the election
And I've since lost track of
Their politics.
Finca
Smoldering the hungry Indians
The dead Green Berets
Like an abstruse variety of
Imported parrots
Determined to prevent
The people from
Minding their own business.
It's tough to dance
To marimba music
If you have as little rhythm left
As the U.S. tourists

That Eisenhower saved the country for
From Communism
One decade ago.

*

They're dancing in the market at Antigua.
The ruins beneath the hand woven blouses
Brown nipples of the early
Flesh age
Brown lips of the babies

Hungry grin
Chemical terror of not enough tortillas.
Bound by chords in their mother's womb
From the lean dark penises
Of their father land,
Balls to beat down
The Roman cathedrals and Texaco rest rooms
Into a shimmering sheet of flesh is
Flesh business
Neither sold nor stolen

From contract to title
But come free to
Spread legs and regard
Fuck or fall back
I love you.

*

Take each others arm in arm.
The old places where the prostitutes
Tits begin
Along the rib cage
Under the arm
Our organs trapped.
The music does not want to die.

Her husky voice ran chills
Up my back
And up and back on my prick.

I said let me sleep with you,
My friend has gone.
We had only together to stay.
I've forgotten your name
But your fucking brown knees
Deep voice
And goodbye

My word
The English
We both knew what it meant.
You said it.
I left.
What little we have left

To prostitute
On the left
Is a staggering brown acreage
Left in the skin trade
Out of their minds
Brown babies, brown balls
Cotton pickers, guides
Labia majorica
Pussy has made

Us all free
By birth
We claim it
Man womban

Organ music.
Let the spirit
Lift up your clothes
And come dancing.

The Oracle of Meth

Through the looking glass with Ben Hiatt
Had put
The mirror off my dresser
On the floor
To get a reflection
Of an impromptu light show
Tied the lantern to the light string
And tried to step
Through the mirror
It looked so deep to him
And I came home stoned
Chased everybody out
Of my apartment.

Broken Mirror
The song sang
Love
For Victor Charlie
Name we gave to a catfish
Caught by Broken Mirror Hiatt
And thrown into the car trunk
All night
And then put in the sink.
It lived that way for days
And we took it to the fountain
At EOC
Put it in the water
And the chemicals killed
It swimmed straight for a while
Then did a few didos
And went belly up

We all went swimming later
In the fountain though
None of us died
But we were not under the water.

Under the influence of
2 cases of beer
3 half gallons of Marco Pete
And 95 capsules of
Methedrine

Split 5 ways
To rap all night
Coming down all over
The next week
Each
At his own
Speed
In the seminar taught by
Famous visiting poet
I'll not mention the name of.

He had given us permission
To enter without paying
The $45 registration fee

And evil eye fleegul
From the business office
Kept after Broken Mirror
Supply and demand
Exceedingly uncomfortable
Bring down.

For Ron Bayes to come back to
Bill Dodd's fuckups
And expect congratulations

For being able to obtain
Paul Engle for $300
One night stand
At *Ars Poetica*
To read his poems
Flex his mussels
Same kind of stud fee
Clam bake
Poetry can be fun.

The busy politicians
Protecting his investment
In the Elk's Club
Didn't know how to go out
With style.

Under the mountain
Afraid of the water
In the La Grande Valley
Grande Ronde River
I rapped all night across the rocks of
5 track mind
High on methedrine and etc.

Grand Ronde Valley
Grand Round Valley
Valley of fatigue
Ground Round
Valley of the great
Circle
Jerk.

Free

4 score and 20 tokes ago
I entered in
To the 4th dimension
And brought the whole room
With me.

The first thing I think of
When I stone is chocolate
Good for tomorrow
When what I really mean
Is my life going to be long enough
To learn
How
Long I can go without
It bothers me sometimes
Women
Surround me as now
I'm into the bag of making
The most important decision
Of my life
Time
Stopped and everything
Was clear.

15 Days in the Middle Class

My mother taught school and my father trapped
Coyotes for the government
And beaver in the beaver house
Used to be a garage.

And so they farmed and things went well.
My father never forgave
The Republicans
Though he knew why
Farmers were so prosperous
Early 1950s
War.

A new white paint job for our house
And secondary buildings.
One time their cabin burned.
But two weeks after application
The paint began to peel
And my dad refused to pay.
Who could blame him.

But he got sued and had to pay
$1100 dollars cash
For the paint job and
The court costs and the lawyer.
It was all downhill from then.

He began to rap at me,
"Get an education son
And your hands on the money,"
As they tricked him
And he tripped me.
Some days I think I'd dig it.

6,000 feet high.
My hands back in the dirt.

My family tried to own two cars.
My brother and my sister split.
They helped me through college.
Nothing worked.
Their marriage paint
Peeled off a white house.

Fu Hexagram 24 No Hangups

Charlie Potts is dead
And I wonder if I should
Be opening his mail
Just as though it had
Been addressed to me
From all his friends

And for him as well as me
I tell you I have gone
All the way with Charlie
Back to nothing
And the cycle is complet
Ed
By the highest sound
I ever heard
Going around in circles
My name is Laffing Water
And whatever form it takes
I have plenty of

Changes to go through
Before I outwrite
All my errors
In longhand Legge's English
10 year trip
With the further suggestive note
10 may be a round
Number
Signifying

Orb
It
Long time
No see

The waiter laid on Crash
In North Vancouver
When we went in to have him
Front us a meal
Chinese English
Keeps my head up
The farthest north
I've been

Though sometimes I feel trapped
With so many other
Ugly Americans
Locked in English
Long time—no see
The blind embrace the blind
The deaf the dumb
The dead the living
Let go of me

I may not be one
With everything
But I am one with me
And you are 2
And we are 3
And 4 is cool
And 5 is plenty
Let's get higher
Let's get higher
One times nothing
Is nothing
Is me
Times it
For it is nothing
And I am it
And everything's nothing
Belongs to you

Are part of it
Doesn't make my difference
Whether or not I'm one
With the phone book
Dial a thought
Psycho somatic music

I'm completely inside
Your head now
But you can relax
For I won't be long
And I'm not dangerous
Nor habit forming
But in case you'd dig to know
Why the sound is coming
Out of your mouth
And into your ears
Ventriloquy
Subtitled
Throwing my voice

You can relax completely now
I'm back in my corner
And it came with me
On the 7th day
It all returns
We got very close to it
Before it got away
But it'll be back
The Sabbath started
With life one and is going
To last 'til dark
Today
As always
'Cause it is
A band of invisible

4 space astral light
We find ourselves
In paradise

Are you ready for this
Have we been here before
But how did it end
It never ends
Mind expansion
The verb for all corrections
Think
About
The petering out of Pleistocene
The sun whips
Guided by
The magnificent completion
Of the next galactic cycle
And the final
Ice age
We passed through
With rudimentary tales
Down the Kelvin scale
Into ground
Zero
Is the round number of
The largest perfect circle
How the genes know
What you all did
Greedy motherfuckers
I can be happy with nothing
Remember
Every step you take
Is in the right direction
And it's not recorded anywhere
If everything is true
This match will sparkle

The police are here to protect the crime. Why didn't anybody say that during the convict strike at San Quentin?
The government of the United States steals more money and kills more people in one day than all the people who have passed, or will pass through its prison system. "Vote for the criminal of your choice." That's Henry Miller. Who are you? Where are you? Registered.

Keep Noah Strate

The unicorns were out fucking
When all the other animals
Were going two by two.
They missed the boat
But don't hold it against them
For being happy.
If Noah had been able
To turn all his brothers on
There wouldn't have been any flood.
150,000 college grads
Don't have to be drafted.
This is prevent a soldier week.
Turn a military unit
Into a human being.
Help stamp out uniform.
Change every mind into a head.
God gave Noah
The rainbow sign
There doesn't have to be
A fire this time.
Rumors of gold pot
At the end.

The *Wild Dog* Distinguished Service Cross
for John Oliver Simon

Let the headlines on the next
Grass Prophet Review
Read
"Laffing Water drops out"

For I simply cannot take
Anybody else's history
Back and forth across
The bridge to print

To quote the Rabbi
In *GPR #5*
"Politics is men distorted by time"
And that includes all the participants
And perceivers who regard it
With anything but horror
And ignore

The kind of liberty
Cleaver will be able to
Get high with guns
To free the blacks
So they can prepare for
Self oppression

And I have been convinced
The United States is over
And the less I have to do with them
The more I'll be able to
Do with myself

I had that trip called concern yourself
With everybody's business
Before my own
Put on me by myself
As well as the most astute

Edward Dorn
Who is as classicists go
A true one
Lover of men
Champion of oppressed people
Defender of lost causes

Whose singular bag of adjectives
Makes music of
What now turns to shit
In my mouth
I give the cross to you
'Cause you helped most
To free me from it
And made me content
With simple undertakings*

It is hard enough
To get out of
Danger
And let the water
Find its way

Forward and back
Across the abyss
To White Knob

Wild Dog
High on Cliff Crik
Aspen leaves
Does anybody remember when. . .

*The WDDSC was taped and broadcast over
KPFA as the finale in a program of responses
from quote responsible community leaders to
Sirhan Bishra Sirhan's application of a
principle dear to my heart, one man, one vote.

Amigo

Hi fast Eddy
This is crying Charlie

From way out West
And a bit down South

And I'd just written
A merciless review
Of the Black Sparrow press
And since I note they're doing
A book of yours
I was wondering if you were still
In England
'Cause I want you to see it.

I remember one time
At the talkathon
On the quote
"Foreign policy"
When you got up and rapped
Everybody out of site
Reading Michael McClure's
Poison Wheat.

But so help me anybody
I can't dig Burroughs.

As I passed through Nogales
A little brown machine
Shat out my ticket
And guess whose name was on it?

There is absolutely no difference
In effect
Between the Nova Police
And the 101st Airborne

And if he really means it
When he says he digs
Rockefeller the first
(*Paris Review* circa 1965)
I don't have to tell you
Whose business
They're protecting.

Cut up language
Has no feeling.
These are not words
On paper
As any non-technical
Language can tell you.
Logic requires
A subject and an object
As Europe begins
About Scottsbluff,
Nebraska,

I heard a classical
Interlude:

Aristotle taught Plato
Turned on
Alexander
As Olson taught Dorn
Turned on
Charlie

And the similarity ends
There
And I continue to be
Obscure and obnoxious

Did you get the books
I sent you
Last fall

For Fascists?

We've begun to chant
Wear motorcycle helmets
And pack a club
There's going to be a big
Peace
Demonstration.

Quote the Way Unquote

So I says to him
'Cause I'm always driving,
Don't stutter
So much

Has come down
Wrong before
We learn

He's not quote
Paranoid
Unquote

But thick mouth never won
Fair syllable.

The way
Is fast
And open

Your mouth
To say
Do you have any idea
How

Much I miss you
Less and
Less now

Words are all
That come
Out of
Your mouth.

A Little Birdie Told Me

I have taken away
Its sound
And you hear it coming at you
Covered with feathers
And beyond control.

I could have loved you when
You put your hand in my crotch
Drunk in church
And high on your own kind
Of trip.

Yours is one
Of the fastest minds
And softest mouths
I hear:

"I wish I were an Oscar Meier Wiener."

Meat demands it
Continue.
My woman woulda killed you
If I'da had one

Dancing alone through Market Street
Where no birds sing

But all night construct
The shock of the heart.

Icarus didn't die.
That is a Greek mistake.
It's impossible to get
Too close to the sun.
He is eating his tail
Only 4 million miles away.
Can you hear?
He digs it.

I saw every fucking star
In the sky tonight.
Icarus is coming
Run for your life.

Icarus is coming
Run for your life.

Little Lord Shiva

The sounds I'm hearing
Are putting me in a trance
From which I may not
Come out alive

Bodhisattvas we
Will not survive
The revolution
In a house in this much dis
Order

When it becomes
Absolutely necessary
I must leave

Apparently only one must die
For no cause
I have done everything
I can except write the last words

Let it be said everywhere
The more who know
The fewer who die
So tell it all

It has begun
And the bells of when
The saints go marching in
With Abraham and Jeremiah
Euripides and Zeus
Lawrence and Ford
Duncan and Whalen
Laffing Water   Laffing Gas

Photosynthesis
I have evaporated
You all are rising
Let each of you cast the first
Stone

The many armed ambiguity
No blame comes
To the sleeping
Abyss

Birth Control

I go striding around Berkeley
With a hardon for 3 days
Now that Laffing Water is
No longer a virgin
But loves as hard as any one.
I rise and rip the city off
My back.

Stoneys are not what I'd call
Happy lover's nuts
Like one of many million sperm
I have found you
And attach myself
To suck all your soft spots
You sway in the mean
Time
I would life you out of
And rap you all the way around
And go to war with your picture
Inside my heart.
Underneath the hand
Woven rainbow shawl
You huddled after love
My queen
It would kill me
If I hurt you.

How sad I was
When your necklace
Broke in my hands.
I pulled the string too hard
But have it swinging
Back around my neck tonight
My rod is hung
Fast and loud and I like it
When you amplify by 10
The forces this electric
Jesus
Is in touch with

Good karma
And it will kill
Everything
If your answer comes back
Anything but
Yes.

The Riot Act

for Edward Smith

About the next time
I almost get run over
By a Cadillac in the
Cross walk
$5,000 dollars worth of tin
Would print a lot of poems
Henry Ford's the name on
The only American revolution
Still going around
The mummy behind
The wheel
       Body by Fisher

Come see
Come saw
We will my when
Americans finally realize
They deserve each other
Let there be no more
Attempted intercourse with the dead
Berkeley babble on
Rubin raps for a yippee circus
"Will we survive Bobby?"
       Who?

It's all politics
They lie
The greatest show on earth
The plague is back in town
To render them
High octane
       Natural gas

Becker showed up in the city
With me and all the other

Farmers
The American migration
Stopped in both directions
The Frontier Thesis
Is a closed book
Maybe you'll be back
In China
Before
    Urban renewal

At 10:00 o'clock some morning cop
Will bum somebody else's trip
And get shot down
One nation
Under siege
There's gold in them thar hills
For those of you who
Make it
    1969ers

I shoulda been a gentle man
I shoulda known etc.
The registered and eligible
And even those prevented
Vote
For something else
I've stopped pretending
To the throne
The people are the people
Their function is to lay
Off us
And give us all the bread we need

Tell them how and turn
Into the rainbow
Hail
And
    Farewell

The Second Coming of Joseph Smith

My life is a tale
Told by women
With bursting ovum
Coming down the fallopian tubes
With their wombs wide open

I've seen my body
Rolled in upon the bed
Hairless and clean
And demanding silence

I am basically
An alimentary tract
Open at both ends
And cared for by a chemistry
Far beyond
My ability to breakdown
And create

Regulated by valves
And an open refrigerator
Though I let myself go
Hungry
To give the edge to my thoughts

The children are happy
With my eyes
As I listen
To each more complex
Tale of woe

Vitamin deficient
And dressed in gifts

I shake my head
And the blood runs out
To the split ends of
My hair
No mamma's boy
And nobody else's
I dance in the streets
When the ambiguous song
Says wait for the women
And don't turn back

I am a Virgo
And I've learned to resent
The extra curricular demands
Made upon my nature

The vision I have
Is a common one
Available to any body
With its eyes wide open
And each of the more
Traumatic events
Puts a layer of new tread
On my brain

And I want only to sing
With my fingers moving
Across the guitar
Fretless and pleased
With the nature of things

It is the story
Transferred by membrane
Or how did the water
Get to the top of the tree

I'm 25%
Impure elements
Brought out of the fire
Eager theologians are impressed by
How long ago it began

By chance
What a hopelessly long
And uneven number
Of light years away
From more sentient beings
Riding a star
In the one true wilderness
Made gross by our lack of
Understanding

The one high
I can't get to
I feel
Trapped in my nature
One chromosome short
Of the equal sign

Uproar and Feedback

Here we are probably seeing a reflection of the
evolution of the brain...the dominant hemisphere
seems completely ignorant of what went on in the other.
However, one hemisphere or the other generally prevails
at any given time. Any incompatible messages coming down
from the other hemisphere must be inhibited or disregarded.

from "The Great Cerebral Commissure"
R. W. Sperry, *Scientific American*
January, 1964

Uproar

for Andy Clausen

I looked into the toilet
and the piss hit the water
and the image broke
and I began to feel
out of touch with everything
and strungout on the profits
of American idealism
as it feeds back and forth
to all brand X Americans
I want your ears without the wax
your undivided attention
and all the money you got
the Bank of America
must be completely
disregarded
to keep you from dying
any sooner than you think
because you can't can't
can't
understand
why I'm sick and fucking
tired of

picking up after
folksingers for McCarthy

Murdock gave his pitch
and it was clear off key
no harmony
no message
he wasn't even keeping
up
with his own time
and split before the poets
had all had their say
Clean Gene is a conscious
agent for
Johnson's schizophrenia
and so many motherfucking
poets keep on writing
with the rite hand
and reaching for the Nobel
Prize with the other
is it any wonder
the rite brain doesn't care
what the left hand is doing
there is a rupture coming
wider than the mark
it will not fit
I've got to
shut up and let it go

2
and so Hitchcock after getting
$10,000 from the man
for *Kayak*
sponsors a little contest
$400 for the best
poem on the subject of
the death of Che Guevara
the theme is madness
style MLA
form preferably sonnet

length is your discretion
scene South America
produced by
20th Century Fox
and directed by the CIA
and it's gonna show up on
Main Street
with all the rest of the pop
corn at the Main Theatre
the other end of which
is the village jail
from which the local
chickenshit
deputy Harold Whitney
sprang so graciously
to let Jerry Wilson
volunteer for the draft
and he got killed
in Vietnam
and from your selective service hands
Wally Kahler
Oval Caskey
Howard Baxter
his blood will not wash off
does it surprise you Mackay, Idaho
that the thin nervous endings
of the selective service system
broke when you reached for me
for I'm a volunteer
from the draft
you carry on in triplicate
and send the children
of the Big Lost River Valley
out to die
for somebody else's
cause
you ain't got one of your own
you twitch
you lie
stranded there

from which I with
eyes on heaven split
and came back for my papers
and got brot down
by your localism
Ox and Hereford and MacAffee
cowboys and farmers
eyes in the front
they ain't got no heads
they lie between the mountains
north northwest
I can't go home again

3
there's a song made lite by the rising
of the dark side of the moon
it's completely invisible
but it keeps their image up
where the tears are never found
in god's eyes

or on my cheeks
'cause I can't cry for dead men
and the living are so few
and full of shit
they pumped our eager heads
and called it love
your country
and your bank account
and so I bought the apple pie
and later named the fountain
after naked Andy Clausen
who ran thru San Jose
and turned everybody on

and 6 people had the lack
of balls
to send their complaints
and tho they got a warrant out
for his arrest

you'll never get your hands on him
'cause you won't believe me
when I tell you
he's completely exposed
all the time

4
and Marvin Garson prints
POETS VOW NOON CITY HALL FOREVER
and clutters up his center spread
with William Blake
how can his schizophrenia go on
the *Express Times*
and Krech could call him also down
for frontpaging
do it yourself sabotage
blow up PG&E
and if he wanted to he would
without broadcasting
mixed intentions
non organic material
is morally neuter
and tho my sympathies
are considerably to the left
I'm politically neuter
and bored with the rhetorical revolution
the Rabbi says the revolution
will set the clock ahead
360 degrees
and I'm rite back where I started
how many times am I gonna hafta
remove
The Complete Tales of Henry James
so we can have a reading
at Shakespeare's Bookstore
and peel layer after layer
of history and literature and bullshit
off my back

I forgive you everything

god bum trips the earth
headlines all over
the 5th Dimensions

and you can't go on imagining
you are in control of everything
you're lucky to have got
a decent potty training
your clothes on rite side out
and something like a woman
to address your deepest
fears and hopes
toward
new ribbons for your typewriter
and life in perpetuity
for the mindless games of
everything
string you out of yourself
with posters and TV
with books and magazines and dope

'cause nothing's gonna save
this place
I used to keep my head free
by allotting only one
mistake per fascist per lifetime
and I'm coming back around
to it
and wish you life indefinitely
and am going anywhere
quiet
to die of my self
inflicted wounds

5
to err is human
to forgive is next
to impossible

for anyone who does not

love
GOD IS DEAD
Nietzsche chortled
because I killed him
makes me happy
and missed out on the good
things in life
no one can do
alone
and tho his head worked
perfectly
there were no next immediate
women in his life
and only the mind could say it
"but your body means well"
there isn't any such thing
as half hi

tho you can be forever
on the way up
and down
and times upon my trips
I've felt I was either
an the bottom or lower
than the ladder goes
beneath it
and above
but those are just no places
I have never been
anywhere but listening to
the rising and the falling
of the tears you're crying
life is very sad
there is no god before me

6
many are called
a few chosen
I was hand picked
the lock off my pants

and rocked back and forth
inside the skin connections
you either got or ain't
and some call it lonely
and some say
that's the breaks
and there are those pretending
to be with it
all the time
and many are
and more ain't
and I begin to see the reasons
for the paramilitary
coup de tete

7
no matter
how far out to lunch
you may sound
as if you knew me
and called me friend
in music
fills the vision
of the universe
I'm writing
and must have
for a while at least
misunderstood its intentions
puncturing the *Litmus* spirit
in the middle of the nite
stapling somebody else's old
poems into history

you're in the room
the floor is rising
and I got my bebe
back

I love everything
forward

and people most of all
wait

what a drag it is
all true
whether I like it or not
but I'm not gonna be
brot down backwards again

and I begin to see the end
of something strung thru outer
space
and nobody seems to realize
how close it is
when Seale secedes from Oakland
and the return burn begins
and the cities crumble into
more obvious piles of trash
and bad breeding inbred
Europe really takes a roll back
and it will be necessary to live
in the country
to survive
no fast war
no obvious bitter ending
years of toil
lie ahead
and hunger and famine and
holocaust
and only the nimble and the sleek
and yes the lucky
species one
ameba to Andy
and everything in between
will go on
much as it was before

and those of us who've ironed
history out
and dug the dirt

and swam thru water
and planted the seeds
and made the bread
and loved the bed

put history in our hands
do it well
and do it quick
the abyss is moving forward
let it take you
don't be afraid
I told the bell bottomed
dungareed young spade
when he asked me if
I'd gone into the other
cave
and we went together
nothing but darkness
nothing like a bottom less
pit with the sound of water
off Point Lobos
and I ran out on the tide
pool
to see if I could tell
where it drained
and they said
"you were lucky"
and I said "no
I could see the wave"
and yes I hurried
and it was slick
but I saw it coming
and got out of the way
and continued my rap down
of the sea lions

ARGHK ARGHK ARGHK ARGHK

and remembered when I dismissed
Henry Miller at Big Sur

for reiterating the bullshit
about rock is nature's perfect
creation
and stood on it as the water
washed its impression
and eventually away
the shingles come clicking
with the sand and foam
and the mountain above Atlantis
broke and fell into the river
I was trying to cross

can you feel the earth quake
and the doctor said
"I'm afraid its diabetes"
and considering how much I care
for sweet things
it was truly a bad dream

and I woke up worried for the sugar
and the insul
ation
I will eat what food I like
and sleep with who and whom
I please
and life goes on
and I get off
a few good rocks
before retiring
to cry my empty heart
with tears for the baby boy
as he stood arms around
the telephone pole
at the Halliday underpass
his been replaced
with the Benton overpass
and the Pocatello House came down
when they cut the trees along the Portneuf
to prepare for a flood
and all my old friends have gone

on their own wobbling trips
and I couldn't even care
for Dawn and Sean and Phil
much less myself
and who am I to worry
for the death of everything
when I can't even keep
all my other selves in place
much less the one that
writes and he who reads
and him whose chief desire
had the day off
and didn't come to see me yet
I know Pat's busy
and I'll hug her when she shows
up
as the whole side
of our better half
and I can't call her anymore
to the co-op on size 11 feet
and pray to move beyond
the dial tone
media is something in between
and I don't want nothing there

9

where all my brothers and sisters
await the end of nite
it's only the beginning
I sang with arms around
Coon and Redboy
drunk on vodka and not giving
a royal shit
about the ice on the street
and the coach's wrath as he
put Coon and I out
2 on 3
and we put down all
the other combinations
he tried to come up with

and derisively referred to us
as the brewery gang
and we just kept winning
'cause we had our heads
together
and he is probly in the mountains
rite at this moment
Crescent Mining Well where he gave me
a place to stay on Bunker Hill's blast furnace
and his dad died doing same
and we became good friends
'cause nobody else could stay
out as late or drink as much
and drive as fast without
getting caught
except the Circle
and we got caught by everything
and women and children and jobs
and Anglo Saxon JDs
don't all vote Republican
as he gave his rite hand twice
when they fingerprinted us
for popping hubcaps
and since he was left handed
they got no impression
and the rite hand does remember
what its left hands were doing
as long as it is done
with nothing else in mind

10
I can't get out of this poem
my head yelled to itself
because the end is arbitrary
based on chance
even with the commissure
sending messages
in all directions

there is no death

because you won't
be able to remember
it

I suppose you remember dying
and coming back to life
and looking back
and fearing the unknown
but you've got to trust it
or die before it happens
which is to say well dressed
cadavers always worry
I do
or used to
but what about
nothing

I see the red lites on the tower
flashing out the window
what is it
that goes on
when all is quiet
and I can't sleep
without it
it's winning again
there's nothing I can do
except sing all the way thru
it

it is it
forward back and verb
it knows yes
to everything
yes to nothing
yes to you
and yes to me
and yes to know
and yes to maybe
and yes to why
and yes to what

and yes to who
and yes to how
and yes to when
and yes to it
and yes to yes
and yes and yes and yes
and

Feedback

for Patricia Parker

dominant   =   subdominant
Language   =   other) sex
          Vibrations

the circle is response
and I don't have anything
to do with it
and ego doesn't matter
'cause we're at the end
of the progressive uptite
that produced the human head
I banish fear with love
and the other rules
the nite
when dry heaves of love and gas
come singing
off the great Cloud of Magellan
and the Tarantula Nebula
and I gather oracles everywhere
from the *Scientific American*
came out on the month
January '64
when I gave up on love
and just got it back tonite
with a transmigratory sympathetic

mescaline body hi
nothing can interrupt
the spinning of the earth
bows down before the sun
and everything is lite again

the Hindu visions of the beginning
was a turtle that carried
the world on its back
and wait
where did the turtle come
from
what turtle
could carry this explosion
between the edges of
begin and end
trapped on earth
'til we surround
ourselves with each's
other
and transcend
the bloody whining
about life and death
those half nouns of
the dark and lite
yin and yang
are easy enuf to draw
but can you make them fit

is the question
when it does its thing
and better than the Christian
vision of hell
puts bad vibes on
my sympathetic nervous system
and you make them go away
I respond and then I move
it must be instantaneous
and I'll put another flower
on my old schizophrenia

as my head comes whole
and ceases to concern itself
with trips other than ours
and everybody knows how
ridiculous

what is love
if not this juncture
where everything's warm and wet
and chewing on each other's flesh
the Eskimos
were in to something good
we sang
rubbing the erectile
tissues in our noses
I can smell you days after
you're gone

love won't wash off
my bebe
my body is absolutely certain
and we slept the dead sleep
having fucked out and off
all our fears
and circle in the afternoon
around a dreamless sleep
in comfort
want my children

I'm more hungup than you are

I sang to you
and you sang it back
and tonite you'll have your home
and I wont even let you let me
out of bed for
poetry and food
are at best second rate
no ungodly matter how hi
can we get

The Total Eclipse of Ezra Pound

1 & it was asked when a man commits murder
By what means should his father protect him
& it replied by all means

2 & Paul X. used to say we gotta get guns 'cause
These mutherfuckers are out to kill us
But since it defined revolution
As the process of destroying the word
Revolution
He now says "We will arm to defend our own"
"Fuck Bobby Kennedy & tonight my weapon is a prick"
& it mingled and furthered with
& when the police & the government disarm
The people will throw down their weapons with joy
There will be no more Fascist duplicity
Soon there will be no more liberals
It suspects all politicians absolutely
& if he wanted to serve his people
He did
& if he wanted to exploit them further
He missed his chance
So be it
The country is in total disorder
& Paul furthered by saying "Mao used the gun
To put down the gun"
Guns are the first thing that have to go

3 & Jan said upon returning from the mountains
I am it looking at itself

4 & it cannot remember a day
When the state was well kept
Nor has it read or heard about one that was
For one that was would truly still be

& when it has utterly refuted history
As it lovingly admonished its sister
If you get trapped in history
There won't be any
There will be nothing
Left to write about & all will sing
As it went on to remind Sunshine
That
If you start anywhere but at the beginning
You won't know how to act at the end
The blossoms on its apricot tree were too many
So it pruned them
& ate the sweet fruit of the many who ripened

5 & it had no children of its own
Yet all children were its by nature
& it stormed heavily at parents everywhere
If you do not listen to the children
They will die everyday of a broken heart

& yet the old man from the straight street world
Came to Shakespeare's seeking the truth
& complained at length
That Hippys would not be straight with him
& it suggested he try masquerade
Get some beads and buttons
& the old man said
He did not like masquerade
& it said dig it
It was about to say
You should let your hair grow long
But that might mean
You would lose your job
& the truth in your case is
Do you want your job more than the truth

6 & it came down on one of its sagest friends

Khoi Phuc
Who preferred to maintain himself in reserve
Saying
Snap out of it stupid
It needs your help

7 & Canto 13 revised by one unlucky
Idaho kid for the other

& it is the same age you are
& came down the mountain between you
Destroying every unholy thing in its way
It is the water
From more than artesian wells
That swells the Pacific Ocean
It flowed into
& no poet worth the verb
Would ever use a Roman Numeral except
As decoration
It does everything as well as it can
Naturally very few know what it means

8 & only when the ears of the ruler are open to it
Wil the state approach the character
Of the unchanging standard
Of constant change
That you translated as order
& Jan said our system projected
To its most efficient
Level
Would not be able to keep up
With the changes
& your weak money bag of statial economics
Has been swept into the sea

9 & Kung did not give the word "order"
But the sound in his mouth that

Is unable to repeat itself
Is the only true
Possibility
Of life after death is nothing
& you've either been there
Or you won't get it
Believe in nothing for it's going to
Save this place & be on time and on top rather
Than in it

10 & it is easier to float
Than to dog paddle or do
The Australian Crawl
& treading water is what
The people who don't know where they're going
Excel at
As charioteering archery public speaking
& basketball
Are inventions by the weak
To entertain and delude with competition with each other
Rather than against the common
Enemy of their incapacity to attain
The real

Take a chariot if you're going long distance
Bend the bow when you intend to kill
& speak in public
When you have anything
That absolutely must be heard

Books are for people
Who like to carry things around
& it's carried *The Cantos* far enough
For the entire civilization is refuted at least
Once a month at the poetry readings and this
Won't be any heavier than it absolutely has to be

The Missing Lynx

Zig Zag

for Richard Krech

Every night I eat
A *ricabarra* candy bar
Chocolate con crema de coco
Nut
And watch my sandals
On the floor
Smoking
Things are for real

Like I met a guy who might have
Come out of a dime novel
Says "You a writer
(I'm returning a typewriter)
And I says
"Yeah, you?"
And he says
"Yeah"

And he'd just got deported
From LA on a grass rap
After 15 years in the US
Got his money and luggage
Stolen in Guadalajara
Which city by the way
Has the most beautiful women
In western North America

I gave him my best shirt
And lend him my favorite
Made in West Germany
And bought in Twin Falls, Idaho
With money I saved
Stacking hay and sleeping in a tool shed

Star Valley, Nevada
1960

He knows the bullfighter dig
Says he can get me in free
First row seats

Hemingway in the distance
Rattling the bones
I sat over one full day
In Ketchum, Idaho
With a full beard wondering
If he really was
Under the concrete slab
Waiting for my father
On the trim grass
I did look
Ridiculous

He was gone with a woman
Trumpets rapping in the bullring
I declined his invitation
And he rapped at me in
Español
Teaching me the language
Told me a poem he wrote
That was pretty good
And just when I thot I'd met
The Mexican Philip Whalen
He says

"I'll see you at the bullfight
I have to go to the Church
And light a candle for the
Virgin of Guadalupe"

And I crashed

Bought a Mexican newspaper
El Costero
Read about all the new music and dancing
Con Ravi Shankar
And wound up watching sunrise
Still stoned and getting
Sympathetic speed vibrations
From a new Canadian friend
Who let me drive his Mercedes
Out to Mismaloya
On January one

Saw a sting ray in the sea
Felt the earth beneath me
Turning still
There are so many stars
When the lights are gone on earth

He said
"One law for the bull
One law for the Matador"

One law for the bull
Ok
But a constitution
For the bullfighter
And 30 helpers to wipe his face
Jab here
Knife there
Horse and picador here
(One bull tipped both horses
Over)
Everybody cheered
The bull got brought down
He was not alone

For r.j. d.a. and the Levites

The word
Game
Has to go

Since I'm not absolutely
Familiar with the details
Of the Willie's visit to Cleveland
You may put him down
For everything
Except being happy

Which he is
And which you ain't
And I'll take bliss
And you can have pain
And presumably when you get enough of it
You'll come off it
And I'll be interested in talking to you
Again

I could have stayed
On the farm and
Complained

La Chartreuse

In a brewery beneath the freeway
At a fashionable party for literati
I spoke for a moment
To a famous middle aged specimen
Wondering where his head was and did
We have any future trip together?

Otherwise,
I crunched on the radishes and potato chips
Conscious of Losing weight.

Then the Rabbi
For he was of the faithful
And clairvoyant,
Loomed over my shoulder and promulgated:
Verlaine shot Rimbaud.

And the faces in french
Lit up with pain
Ful flowering syphilitics.

I looked back at the Rabbi
Standing on El Diablo mountain with
The mist moving between his fingers
And his family and said:

Yeah,
But he didn't kill him.

Inside Out Upside Down and Backwards

My goal is to become the world's
Most perfectly developed nihilist
My plans are few
And far between

I reiterate
My hypothesis
That where we were before
Cannot be seen

By the naked eyes I fastened
On the stairs
A corps perdu
And sitting at the table said:

If I don't die
In the next five days
Everything is gonna be all right

Then looking into the aghast
Faces of my assembled friends replied:

If I do die in the next five days
Everything is gonna be all right
Anyway

Amidst their relief I must admit
I am less than desperately
Increasing on the passive

I even lack credentials
And go seemingly to slip
Myself upon the list of things
I can do without

Confessing schizophrenia
And have been known occasionally to flip
A glance of stark disdain

The Daily News

for Max Scheer

For William Randolph Sheer
Gall and stupidity
Overrides what sense
Your *Berkeley Barb* makes.
You've got to meet your dead
Line
Pushing out the news,
None of which is
Fit to print.
On Tuesday I'm not dying
But on Friday
I am.
Hear me out
No news
Is good news.
It's past
Time for
The truth.

I read that stack of shit
Submitted to your paper
Looking very much like poems
On the page
But sounding out of touch
With anything for real,
One poem of 300
Worth the printing
"Minh Ti's Ear Rings"
With the sound
None of you hung studs
Seeking same
Can get to

Or away from.
Your swap ass ads
Are dumb
Laid out by all the gory
Details of your bank account
Which next to mine
Is fat
That will be trimmed away.

The revolution is
Access to the media
By those who have nothing
To lose
And the most
To say.
You want to do a supplement
And be a sugar daddy?
I'm not interested
In patron
Izing anyone
And supplement is
Another way of death
And divorce
Is what you all went through
Stuck up
In the plastic
Vending box
Between *The Chronicle*
And *The Gazette.*
The open whore of horror
Spreads her metal legs
And you all fall in
Line.

The stupid sad uncertain
March of the tele

Type,
The language
You all never speak
Or sing
But only read and shudder.
United Press International
Controls your every move.
You die like disenfranchised
Paper men.
Gutenberg is over.
The page is blank and wasted
With the words you seek to
Correct it by
And by
The bay will fill
With mud and blood
And they will say
In squarer circles
The Berkeley Barb
Is alive in Argentina
The myth
Ical home
For most retired
And retreaded Fascists
Can't think
Of anything to say.

And so report the news
Of death as it gets closer
And they are putting up another
Bank of Ameri
Card
On the street
Where you live
And precious little
Credit's due to

All the empty heads
Blown down Telegraph
Or any other God
Forsaken Avenue
Where they smash the Jabberwock
In one full day of dozing
Bull.
The sign across its soon
To be no more out front
Said:
Values,
Which is to say the Jabberwock
Had more lasting structure
Than any institution
In this country.

Poets used to sing there
About the lonely days and nights
Of not being
Listened to.
The glaciers will rise and overrule
All of California
And other minds and thoughts
Will occupy
The dead
Space
Along the concentric lines
My sound moves out on
At the speed of God
And through you no more than by
The rattling bones
Inside your middle ear.
I'm aiming at your head
Which may be shrunk
As though I were a Jivaro
And packed upon a stick

For neither time nor age
Is important measured
By the calendar
As the months and days and hours
Go around
But not by
Me
For I'm not for sale
And intend to borrow
A broom to beat
A lot of sacred shit
From so called revolutionary
Cows with
And put the ones whose minds cannot be
Changed
Out to pasture
As you go home to lunch
And out to
Like a light
And I go over
To a different friend's house each night
And am delighted by the bread
They break with me.

And as the fires start again
From Boston to LA
I used to sing
The sacred rock and roll
The boat
Peter Pan flew out on
From Disneyland with Tinkerbell
And almost all the other
Angels and dwarfs
Applauded
Disney's creativity
And plastic was pumped

Through everybody's tubes
To better preserve
The loss of vitamins
E and K
Shows on your face as well
As the face of your rag.

Which Dr. Leary
Are you talking
About
Love?
Welcome to UC Berkeley
Now you don't
Make much sense.
We've heard a lot
About you
But not much from you.
Ian Fleming is a stupid writer.
You repeat a couple of
His worst mistakes
And *The Barb* reprints it all
From *The Seed*,
5 times away from the truth
And they call it a
Gag.

I hear it said you want
To turn straight
People on
And people off
The beaten brain waves
Journalese travels on
Say you're hurting
And I agree
With both and everything
And don't want you to
Die in their sleep.

Hello Bebe

Hello Bebe
I will say
When next our eyes
Locked on to it
And eager fingers trace the edge
Our genes have made for us
The central nervous system
And gathered everything I want
Inside of you
The wet way love will open
Both of us up again
I can't live without you
Shimmering gift of a natural growth
I'll eat everything you bring me
And guilt goes slinking
Further and further
Away from us
From you
The halves of us not interested
In getting deeply involved
Go out and make a whole
In some other place the love
Has no desire to get to
And the halves of each
That demand the other
Making fucking such a central dance
There's no need to control
My joy
I will come when time is right
And fill you gentle woman
Clothes off
Lips on
The other's trembling bag of skin
Made hard by all unhappiness
And opened out
By love

Empty From the Navel Up

What if I never see you again?
And my head goes blank
Where the terror grabs me
And I've been taught to disregard
My root rising at the base of things
My mind has been quote blown
And I am empty from the navel up
What children joys and fears
Await us
Driving through
The dead god's town
Oakland, California
Circa 1968
I can't believe
You won't come back
I'm ready to do anything
I can't do nothing
Without you

Uptight Head Tries Thinking Out

My head stares through my eyes
At my reflection in the toilet
And the piss hit the water
And the image broke
And it all began to sing
Where are you
That
Our faces trained
For good and ill
Should force a simultaneous
Smile
On the lips go tremble
For lack of you
And nobody else is here
Or there
Inside my all too sluffoffable
Skin
Peeling back perimeters
Looking for the real
Center of things to carry me
Heart is on the edge of things
And uptight head tries thinking out
No desperate measure disallowed
Against
The failure of my trip
You are both reason and reward
And still it
Can't be controlled
On the clean floor I have swept
The ashes up
And I am carried by size eleven feet
Far beyond the dial tone.

The First Part of the Past

It's incredibly difficult
To refer to only the first
Part of the past

Imagine a muglet

Make no mistake
Johnson was not
The angel of death
Passing over
You
Have just begun
To die

We are the soldiers of the rainbow
I told you my left hand
Couldn't remember

I talked my old lady
Into giving me a blowjob
While I'm writing
To see if it works

The List

The list of things that are fucking my head:

Pat

> "The first evil is that
> Which has power over you"

Has my lover forgotten
Where I live
That the chemistry rises
Solely for her pleasure
Has her husband hung her up
Her job
Did she make a good trip to
Palo Alto
Does she love me
As she pretends
Should I worry
Or are we friends
It's a lover's question
I'd like to know

Soul

So now it's the point
And I violated
All 10 Commandments
With one erection

Soul:
My body was
Fighting with my mind
And it one

Salvage

Now I cling to the legs of 2 married women
queer for the teenager in Levi's
after the adultery and his cowboy boots
bad dreams and hand jobs
steadily shrinking bank account and waistline
drugged friends with hebefrenic grins
passing out in mid air
leaflets of the malaise
down with everything and up with me

Thumb job onto raked corvair
hungover mechanic headed for San Francisco
tuned into K farce and "The Secret
Agent, Man" is shotgun dum founded
alongside the long way home
thru the Oakland hills
jitterbugs in Moroccan fez
skirts and silver handled pistols
pass thru the atmosphere

All chained all hell all waiting
for the next worthwhile thing
crying over food kool aid
the director insisted on keeping
wet on, eyes opaline for
some crummy never do well messiah
who never showed up
his curly hair ingrown
toe nails reserve the rite to dismanipulate
himself wired to herself
their selves spinning on down
contradiction in terms
of the burr headed bureaucrat
up a eucalyptus with a printing press
demanding obeisance to the way
I'm here to witness the crime
what crime

the crime your not knowing what crime
makes you a part of
puzzle it out you finks
I've met for a fat friend who left me in
your clutches, thinking he put you down
but hit me instead

The bay area floats from the rafters
looking down on the clouds the fleecy
pollution we have come to know and love
is the key that wont turn the lock
either way you chose to die by trying
or die earlier by telling them straight
you bore me can it shove off

Exchange of nectarines
young lady I could have straddled
looking for the *Barb* office
I walked her too much later telling the
overworked over-egoed over ran editor
to read us and not Dostoevsky
handing him a *Litmus* as he claims
to be getting old, I say if you live
rite you'll never grow old

Spare rib kitchen green mansions
once thrived poets in panchos
drifting gayward out of the arms
of the whore of Babylon into rope lent
and never returned enuf to hang him black self
chip of hash for a few lid turn on
howling down the walkway
women over his shoulder pleased with me
for being the last to look out
we could have gotten along even better

Cheap red balloon she said what happened
it is broke
no you popped it
should have sooner shook tramp tramp

tramp of the mysterious thunderbird
his mulatto tendencies trying to scare
me with halfa spook and guns galore
shep old dog he probly nutted down
with when his friends or creditors
weren't on his just too private line

No more way out tea shirt and jeans
and big eyes for how I am trying
all nite to avoid tho tantalized I went
rite in 6 weeks later, St. Vitus dance
thot I could worm out with footsy wound up
getting hard myself then naked when
the sun cried the baby up and I tho dreaming
I am dead am relatively free tho who dare
die hard on worse than being run over
by a truck with a fat wallet and an empty
stomach so she comes back I part those
heavy slices

Dont tip the candle over get up
off the floor the bubble machine
had drowned the glide is no more
America than you wont let go of so
why doncha worry more about how you are
and less about how they take it

Hopping up and down with crab grass on my
balls a small fire of post coital very
reluctance squatted on the door with a few
other syphilitic pregnant speed freaked out
and just plain weird hippies waiting for
the flash of the good doctors stethoscope
at the free clinic on the corner of
dog shit and psychedelic

Waiting for the chariot of the moon
to whisk me off to misunderstandings
by the sea
fat bald father of Siamese twins

his cat splayed the mattress full of
fledgling pussies sometimes thot of as
kittens as the pussy proper came and went
remember me he hypothesized
to faces wrenched into their own make
believe make do symbolism

Still alone at this time just as scared
as he always was will be I hate to say
snap into karma control, it with your
attitude I am not Norman Vincent Peale
nor any reasonable facsimile thereof
however if you persist in paranoid
something bad is going to happen to everybody
and then you'll say I told you so
see how warped you can get
think of union 76 union jack
united fruit to end the hypocrisy
of occult dodgers on the literal
problems faced with no happy ending

At last I've thot long enuf to construct a line unprintable
by density is value cubed into pictures no more epicentrific
poetry with dual referents and resulting single dimensions or
even hypo centrific by the addition of depth to latitude
and longitude this is 3 but we're leaving it for the one
world izm of the 4th congratulations of Mahamudra
all I ask of the world at large is consistency of result
which it is powerless to deny me if my theories will bear
the scrutiny I apply, see it's all unique to itself nothing
will come on any way except how it can and given
poverty of the imagination, I've had the course, the world is a
captive of the short track minds making up the
bills of lading the bills of attainder the bills of duck
billed platypuses rushed on stage at the last act to
marsupial you all into believing nature has any imagination
greater than need
sometimes thot of as the shifting face of all desire
went down on it wif his mouf as per her strangled cry
and picked from his teeth the bleeding gums he sucks

until this day and spits blood across the garden
black and holy wind mill boobies I sucked until
she could no longer stand it ragged and bleeding guilt
tried to blow it but primary impetus was lagging
I just eat pussy because not to do so is duller than
what I'm doing now—all basic bodily functions
quite intact in spite of the grisly business here at hand:
all poets are liars; great poets are liars with such impeccable gift
you think you're hearing the truth when what you actually hear
are little psychic log jams breaking up in your head

Herein I place the
gram of diplomacy Timothy shit his pants on why
the rug should be on the floor and not the ceiling I won't say
I plan to live to be 94 years old is exactly what the opium
thot most pertinently to tell me as i skedaddled down
the ave. giving skin to every wayward spade whose psalms
we crossed in stupifactioned glee
it is no service to deny me my hour on the sun
cut short by the quivering thighs of ladies wrapped in under
garments on the underground tour, fortunately there is no jazz
to speak of, fat girl hitchhiker pubes poking at me
to prunce or denounce the shit I took and constipated laid up
an inside prostate job massage and the white boy cried so
hard there was what home to come to
in all this muckraking turned over shit before the dung
beetles have done all their discouraging work
we said against the preciousness of a little more time
por favor! because all those gestures did mean something
else than what they seemed and swept up
coke cups whiskey around co-deine hi we
carried that rack down Telegraf and Hippys
stared who are ordinarily so cool you could see them off
on some poor girl who hit me for some free money
I said here's some free poetry offering her a *Grass
Prophet Review*, and she said no thanx and tho it's true
you can't eat poetry still I had the presence of mind to
offer well in that case, I will fuck you for a dollar

So J poet lost the book of changes Rabbi's phlegm to rage

it being his copy of the book absent mindedness
poor Andy wailing all all alone almost always
had more to say than the few who stopped to listen
could take in his misery in the middle of a fite
with Linda morosely so, says I think I'll be queer for a while
and J poet contradicted him in the back of the Rabbi's
remodeled chariot of Sears van with you think they always
get along too huh. And J poet and I double timed a stranger
lady got enuf for fruit and candy on the street
where you live

There are joys none the less barefoot and belled up to the walkway
on my door from Big Sur-Venice in this city without walls
chiefly eating pie or pussy and variations on the same old routine
Edy said "everything I do, I do every day," the rhythm of the sage
made mandatory on the housewife role she felt trapped in
holding shy hot little hands with the beautiful man who told me
what she needed
innocence was how I feigned

Looking out the window into rainbow over sprinkler
there is no cause for alarm tho strange nudes walked
back and forth with labrador retrievers nose almost on
the money when Hiatt brot the Vagabonds into my
room to leer such peeping petty toms across the
2 story hi drive way of the confused pleasures of the flesh

It was here the spiders crawled at nite with razors in their teeth
with the clik clik clik clikking of the intricate locks people out of
love
put on their doors and the music failed to lift them so
she put on the rainbow shawl and the soft unmatched
leather driving gloves and rodded her little MG back and
forth across town, bought me buckwheat pancakes rite
after I stripped my room of all the disentanglements
posters and flim flam I had chosen to become
blank as the oracle in and table table table the rosa'll
she came rite into and getting fucked by each other was
why we were there together assholes winking side by each
a little sweat and glaze over the eyes of love

You wanna see my chicken the picanniny proffered rite on
or near Easter I stepped into his house and in the cardboard
box a little yellow peeper scratched on paper with a saucer
flying full of food and tuna can of water, nice bird I flew
up and down those streets in flat footed sandals flat stomach
do to intake into the market for my daily payday candy
bar and apple I got what nourishment there was to be had from

I bought another apple crossing Castro in the dark sipping wine
with drunken natives in the doors of bistros on the way to putting
down the black sailors who tried to razz the man who
handed me the wine
in that zook suit honey, I'd be ashamed to walk the streets

Next day poking fun at hard hats chugging up the dirt
on psychedelic street suggesting that it looked deliberately
like the war zone it was to become why doncha dig
a hole and fall in it

the peace and freedom party implied little of the same
old rigmarole once their signatures propel them onto
the so-called ballot we went investigating precinct 11
I believe in the gym of a grade school burrheads
cross swords on such hallowed ground as
I've heard all the Sproul Plaza rhetoric I care to
and Paul X would jump up and talk about guns
and Richard made a few saner points I tried to talk
the women chairman of the resources i.e. finance
committee into levying a tax on dealers to ten percent
to include the legalization of weed in the platform
All I really got was a brief friendship with a latent panther
and the earphones of Leon and Suzy where I chuckled to myself
chiefly across the indecipherable strains of "The Drifter's Escape"

History Repeating Itself

What I know about history is that it doesnt make any difference
what makes a difference but I wont answer questions except
one you think good enuf for me I wasnt bullshitting any
body about the boredom but
it had a desirable effect which is
exase which exase them both from
the memory by understand as much of all the data
coming in as you can pan handle anybody with music like this

outrageous drunk thot he saw a fellow spirit
wanted a dime pushing with his hands
"fuck you" walked on by the lite in and out side of him
since he'd lost his shadow, but the drunk cat tried again
I was eating an apple, "at least you could give me a bite of your
apple," I did an about face, plunged closely to his teeth
hissed EAT, the apple clutched in my rite paw and dragged
it back as quick as he shook my hands said "I'm Bob." "I know,
I'm the 2nd continual coming of Sitting Bull"—shit how else are
you gonna keep it all clean—shock the heart, I span spun spin
'ed away and walked on the whole performance taking less than
10 seconds so listen with remember how many feet about 4 of
course—
jay walking over a chicks rap "Christ died for..." "Sitting
Bull didnt die—he listened up for another 100 hours on natural
speed

Water? probly the hydrogen and the oxygen (chuckles) Laffing

Water tried to keep me from reading—I stood my ground—he
dragged the carcass tord the sea see cork ass floats around
blank hole in the side a spring blue ball inside a red one
spin inside the others all spinning in totally opposite
directions, particularized directions of the reversible rain
bow, now you see it now you dont—great erase it.
stem and all"

The doorbell rang on rainbow, and Blazek was explaining to Kryss

105

who had just come in that I was making a tape,
Blazek chuckling in the background.
"I was mad, I was mad, I was mad,
I was mad, I'm not mad any longer."

(The End)

mirror mirror on the wall
what
is furthest out of all

the lite came back on
Earl Warren used to be governor of California
he was as good as the marshall plan or better
than most
he and the meat
Cleaver
know 2 much
this cockroach is quivering like the blue
life you'd think I'da been taking dope
must be about time for the tremor
its watching me rite now
just
ran away
6 legs times you know how fast that is
I tried to sleep took it away from it
self put it back in my heart like always
baby a little star to carry around with me
and a face with more wrinkles
than you can imagine constantlee
shock of the heart
attack
change so
try it
how
sleep, & find out

the end 1
the universe is blank strung together with "ofs"
you know better will you learn in time

fast out
the eggs are breaking down the shells of it
flies are buzzing everywhere
the fastest verbs in town
I got this brother see
Don Gray tomorrow nite and learn about
the witches in the south of Yeats
he may do my book in red
my role is to make
the best better than continual improvement
SADIST they screamed
the cockroach is shaking again
I'm sorry I killed the other one
it made it
scurry away on all sixes
grasshoppers cream de minths what
have you 2 lose
I'm teaching this little bird
to fly in air as
well is water
chickenshit canary

the end too 2 end
whistles thru a golden cage
atonal screams before they real
eyesd it
is trying hard not to hurt them
the little sparrows at the end
of my unpolished finger nails demand
England etc.
pan am
bonanza, fools gold, iron pie rite,
el matadora
straight thru the bulls neck red blood
warbles how true
get higher can't see the uneven
edges on the red corpuscles
useless pus rid ic ul ous ridik
and ridik again
old

Mexico
cherries ripe rong what have you
good to eat
Dave is via Buffalo
can you make the connexion how
to not die
siteless whirring in the hot
water tap I rapped back
everybody else is relaxed
can you
stay out of the red plane
this is your brother with an R-H negative factor speaking
sterility of Sitting Bull is eclipsed by
fecundity of the second continual coming
I blew the cockroach in a horse shoe
spiral clear out of trembling
he's up on the speaker now
trusts me completely

3
that is was the wind of death
& hustled to whatever
the fuck it is cockroaches think about
baffled me for a second
got it

so I got this brother see
up in north eastern Nevada
rancher few cows
horses up the yingee
flies around town on his red
paper air plane feet
wanna bet about the title
I havent had more than 10 hours of sleep in 100 hours
or maybe more I have forgotten how
to sleep
believe it or else
the bets off
massaging as many of the stopped
hearts as I care for and am able to

get 2 first every time I start to
count hurry or you'll miss it
scars
are healed wounds the young teach the
young I'm the same age as what's
his face doing now

4
rubbing his neck
the sleep out of his eyes is four
the horses that carried it away
Andy
Khoi Phuc
Ben
Joel

tonite I'm looking straight thru
the back of the head in each witch
every 4 tunes rich
faster faster faster teach them
how the wood feels on the saw
I'm sitting on shellac
La Brea struck down
the pot and the Trojan mother
Shakespeare's best lines
ras yr ras yr ras yr ras ras ras ras ras ras ras
Jamaica are unrepeatablc
this is the tarantula under glass
2 more legs than the cock roach
dont multiply imaginary possibilities
stick to the real sense you make
of it
what you want
the cockroach is waving his brain
antennae from the toe
of witch foot the farrier holds
you first

5
the siren I heard walking out of

the mission to the hate
was cool
blew the warm hot shit of Sitting
Bull over 20 faces
changed an other
half our episode remains
to be seen
the cockroach went over the back of the chair
if there are more than one
cockroach we the 8 fastest feet
of the tarantula
will never finish the *Litmus*

I have killed one already
the cockroach pain is upon me
that one was a long horn in my heart
the man who gave me the ring
with the 12 hand made changes
that I spin tears from the
dark between the hairs
lost its face
lose yours again and again

6
will be faster
the genius of more than 6 overlaid layers
of mask is weaving wearing me to a
frazzle of horse to the sixth
working in all directions tord
new havens for the lite and water drops
of bullshit
from the rainbow
song springs forth hi in
the air
quicksilver is faster than fools
gold the floor can't seem to remember
why it got in the way of
spiral
            taps
                    left left

                    tom tom
                         thumb
makes the holy hollow wood rise again
the walls creak
the roaches come and go on
this cushion of air hi
above it
pan has cloven webbed feet

7
crossed hap hazardly from
what you all ready know tarantula
spirals a hex on bannannans
united fruit company love
the eyes that see straight thru
remember the medulla oblong
got ta, got ta, got ta,
St. Gertrude was a great cook
pan ran away with her white bones

Sitting Bull remembers to raise
and lower his legs in order to keep
the hot blood moving to capsize
held in the air delirium
heavy heavy breathing in the throat he cried
when I walked his fat little body to
the scales
25 & 1/2
cents a pound lb lb lb lb lb jay?
lips twang in both cars at once
the floor dropped considerably
both and on tip toes
the blood red web of the hour glass I'm under from the
red belly of Mary will be washed red on
red off red on red off, clean

8
where'd he go, bullshit rides again
hot air—fart face
there is no deceit when the mask gushed

from outside thru the blank center and
hangs up on the chemistry
Brahmin is a natural
so is shorthorn
Santa Gertrudis was invented on the
king ranch out in Texas
Sitting Bull is 3 changing are inches give or
take the waves see below the Sur
face of it
       Santa Gertrudis is in deep
in the blood blood blood blood
of the changing living land equals balance
solid hard line hard place gate
neither of horn nor pearl nor any
more homemade mistakes
the great gene crossing to blank occurred
Kent, Kemp, whew!

be (9) by nature by nature I hurry
having got as much of
the shit out of my mouth at once
as lite comes once more to the wide awake
outloud sleeping dreamer behind
mask to the 4th and left of that
the shit is about to hit the fan
and when it does believe dont
get hungup in its trance
I always wanted to be an epileptic
with water on the brain
I can cure it with a drink
went barefoot in cocoon
star fish feet warm no koff koff
for hours again
the biggest shit of the major
generalizations on this continent
has no one name the others can recognize themselves
fairly clearly, Lawrence saw only
what he wanted to see

10*
the Chinese water torture
bird eyes for real
the falcon is for him
the blood goes around the body
of the black widow
spinning along on his back under
the floor regarding the blue
epileptic spoke he's traveling thru
the sport of chinese water
kings X
on your face / forehead making a
weird looking circle of the
unicorn's blank spot made of
shimmering beams of lite
neither holding
neither contracting
older than Yeats flippeding out
shit straight in the air
vampire of the rue
de la rue
on the street
where you live
                morgue
go gone go gone go gold go water
Sean Sean
the spider spins again

"Bizarre," spare change, I asked you for a quarter of an hour.
Tape it was your response, you went to Sur, catch as catch can.
−Square deal composition property of Laffing Water, subject
laffing gass, price 49 cents. For Harry Truman, and Julia Newman.

This poem is for my
crab spider and
all the flies
blue lite
I covered all the bases and pulled
the diamond out from under him
crystal ball with 58 plus

his own face
love
de
vine
your HEAD
or the hunters
will get it

"The Trancemigraçion of Menzu: The Parody of it"

It is the other
side of Noah
laff a lot
Andy, devine
for it is also called
jazz jizz ummmmmm
the last introduction applause etc.
it is also a parody of
Ravi Shankar
Socrates or Aristotle or
the TRUTH
either even
Sousa and Bee
thoven
Eldridge and Reece
Ricky Nelson & Lord Byron
Olson or Creeley or Dorn
and it
cash and, Johnny Cash, Johnny Cash
cash, cash, cash, cash for Dylan Thomas
cash and Eliot
both and Handy's
ears & hands
both and
Ayler and Lloyd
and coal train
Tennessee ear nest
Ford & Chevy & shimmy
Madox
Ford

d volks everywhere
n use a decent wagon
ngue take me up for
ao & Ike
general to be
ecific
rivate Eddy Slovik
rivate enter
rize
e Nobel is dynamite
ow it up 2 and
op
e bag of ill wind
AMIKAZE RAINBOW STAR DIVINE
HE HOLE
OATLOAD OF XYLEM PEOPLE
hope I havent forgotten anything important
ng and old and Freud and all
e immortal living as we do
ever ate the rest
need sleep 2
merous to mention
hakespeare
it it only if YOU absolutely have to
elieve it or else
eloved
      VANISH

'm worried, I havent heard from Vanish, he has heavy changes to
o thru in August. He wanted to be my lieutenant, 'cause I was
ways asking him questions and he said, how can I give you all the
te answers it you dont ask me all the rong questions? And I
oked back into his eyes and said, if you practice," I said dropping
it of the text of the poems I was reading.

LASH FLOOD pocket pool of
racles miracles and what have you

4 - 8 Pat saved HEAVEN
it is a drag some times Dawn
does not come between the middle
over the edge
round the corner
peeks at you
from the east vague other
gift of gab
policeman who only gave me a warning
ticket after speeding and picking up 2
hitchhikers *North to Alaska* and
Beyond the Fringe
go gone 1945 face of it
FACE THE MUSIC
Zig swam across
both directions
American Falls
reservoir is silting full of sand
portige
all my Marys
I have rejected Hankir Vidrandi
psst Andy
Attila the Hun is alive and well
in Los Angeles
THE COMPLETE WORKS OF SHAKESPEARE
ARE A HISTORY COLLAGE WHO NEEDS IT
AND THE BIBLE THE BOOK OF
WORDS WORDS WORDS
'THE GURRY OF IT'
TANSI TANSI TANSI
ONLY THE SOUND IS TRUE
PEGASUS FLEW AWAY
WHERE IS IT NOW
eating snow is fun
going home, (snapping fingers and singing), going home, going
home, going home, to see, to sea, with 5 sense plus 2. 4 1 in 10, 9,
8, 63, Ada Marlene Menzu, Menzu, Menzu, I love you, I love you
I love you, Menzu, Menzu, (blubbering), I love you, I love you
Menzu, I love you, Menzu, I love you, come back Menzu, I love
you Menzu, I love you, please come back, I love you, star star star

star star star star star star.... Khoi Phuc,
coy fuck it all."
        "You wanna take a break man?" Blazek interjected.
"No, I'm too hi."

3
Topsy part II
the tiger at the top
of the changing line
plunged ahead
of the *lit er ati*
and pounced on Meitraya
grasping his chubby hand
in both claws
and later curled up
at his feet
to listen
to the music coming out
of his mouth
said you're not supposed to
do the *Ching*
'til you're 50
poetry aint great
'til it's been around
for a 100 years
pooooooooooooof

Flower child of Black Mountain beehive
if the buzz saw
gets into your head before see
you're too young
to handle
it
sing back to the little ones
for them the sting
must be spontaneously
filled love
forget it

Sarah
the nuclear
nocturnal emission
last nite
unable to sleep
it happened
again
the book
of changes says HEED
AFTER 3 WARNINGS
WORRY WORT THAT I AM
I DANCE OVER THE EDGE
OF PANIC ON TO
THE ICE
AT THE SPEED OF LITE
GOING THRU ON ALL 4s
CHANGES WITH MY LAST
DESPERATE ATTEMPT IN
ALL DIRECTIONS AT ONCE
TO ACHIEVE THE FINAL
FORM OF IT WITH
THE BRILLIANCE YOUR HEAD
GAVE ME TEARS
BEFORE IT HAPPENED
MOMMA
I PUT MY FINGER
ON MY NAVEL
FELT MY HEART
BEATING THERE
REMEMBERED YOU
REMEMBERED POLLY
AND WENT TO SLEEP
ARCO
forget it

(sniffles) I want my momma to change, I want my momma to
change, change, change of love, has got a hold on you, and it ai
the kind, that you can lose, this change of love, has got a hold o
you. Khoi Phuc.

118

The Straits of Magellan
yogi bear
ambled down 21
getting higher and higher
forgot
where he was
looked back
no H, the fifth note
has been around the world once
I shook my shadow
and the hair danced the concrete
on back up
forget it

The tiger is lord
of the beastly spirit
coming thru India
and China and into the *I Ching*
and thru the German language
into English
it renders everything
the panther is leopard
of the craftiest defense possible

and brot his boss black coat

from Folsom changing
heroes in mid abyss
backwards into grass
on the black continent
to the point*
we have genes in common
on back
the forward
spiral

(H20)

FLASH in the Pan
it is correct for alto than thou Duncan to say

"Litmus is unremittingly heterosexual"
and when next my eyes fall upon his
I will say
it further is bisexual
auto erotic
this section 8 in all is my ego trip
self protection
all the rest of them
are for you
our thing is in the head
it would break my heart again
to say no to you
we are too happy for Lot's tears
forget it

R.C. Lion
David Bromige
this hurt me as much as it will hurt you
but it has destroyed the word
only the sound remains are music
there is no end quote

Maya on New England errr
Laffing Water of everywhere to Maximus of Gloucester can yo
hear me come in please roger over and out
Laffing Gass of everywhere to Maximus of Gloucester can you
hear me come in please roger over and out
Ice Water of everywhere to Maximus of Gloucester can you he
me come in please roger over and out
so it asked you 3 times and still no response
it is only one of the contemporaries you sang about and said
"hail them, and watch out"
hail to you 2 out of touch with it but be advised we're here to
destroy history not to read it and there is only one way to impr
language by using it and the syllable came from outer and inner
space from Shakespeare to Pound to me bla bla and it ran it bac
over all of you

the most sense you ever made was a paraphrase of Bernard de
DeVoto to the effect that a mountain man has the best available

sense in America and it's rite and my father is and it is
and it'd rather hear from him than from you any day now my
country is of the Pacific spirit and stops at the great
divide
Massachusetts is nowhere, included
like it got a request for a free sample of *Litmus* from your alma
mater and threw it away and later gambled a 10 cent stamp on a
5 dollar bill its got nothing to lose and hallucinated a letter as
follows:
Dear Harvard
to who it may concern
I'll trade a sample of *Litmus* for a sample of a full ride scholar-
ship, it dont wanna take any classes or nothing but you are by
reputation the greatest university in the civilization and it just
wanna come and hang around for a year and see if you're doing
anything important.
it never wrote the letter, like it said, Massachusetts, is not in my
country, arrivederci Europe
forget it faster
I love you special with R. W. Sperry no time to explain

Notes tord a proper movement, the River of no Return... make it
the rice is cold, I'm still hungry, make your own copy of it today
free,
sandskrit...Chairman Mao mau mau mau.

Aztec Reflector

They're going back to Xochimilco
On the same road that they came
And they're bringing lots of flowers back
That they picked in the rain
Their hair is long their eyes hang blue
Their faces are screwed with pain
They're wondering why the war don't stop
And they're looking for someone to blame.

It will look all alike much later
When peace breeds another war
And they'll advertise their scars and laugh
At what they're fighting for
The speed is set the game is go
And they don't really try to bore
But these smiling dead young androgynes
Don't even keep score.

Their love is gone they live on hash
Their lives are not the same
They question and feel guilty that
Their parents are not sane
They wear no shoes and realize
Their protest are in vain
The cold ribbed push of fear enslaves
Everything they claim.

The Return of Laffing Water

I woulda been back sooner
If I'da known that I'd been gone.
The last time I seen her
It's been far too long.
I love every change she makes
I want her by my side
But she is married to another man
And I sit at home and cry.

Laffing Water in the wilderness
Is calling me home
But I can't leave without her
And I can't go on alone.

Tell me where her head is
About all important things.
I can promise to not hurt her
As long as everybody sings.

Water in the Wilderness
Just dropped his adjective.
The tears rolled down my smile
And the whole world grieves.

The Road to Charlie's House

The road to Charlie's house is marked
With only one restriction:
It's rumored Charlie died last night
And the rest is superstition.

I gave him all the love I had
I swore across his fear.
But there is no time for a funeral now
I'm one with all the years,

That preceded me and stretch out front
From life one until dark.
And he was cool part of the time
Was paranoid of narks.

He got busted once too hard
Into a million pieces
And ants came dancing 2 by 6
And overran his species.

I'll sing their song with a loud guitar
My voice again tonight.
Charlie's rainbow broke a last
And everything is light.